Seeing yourself through the eyes of a camera!

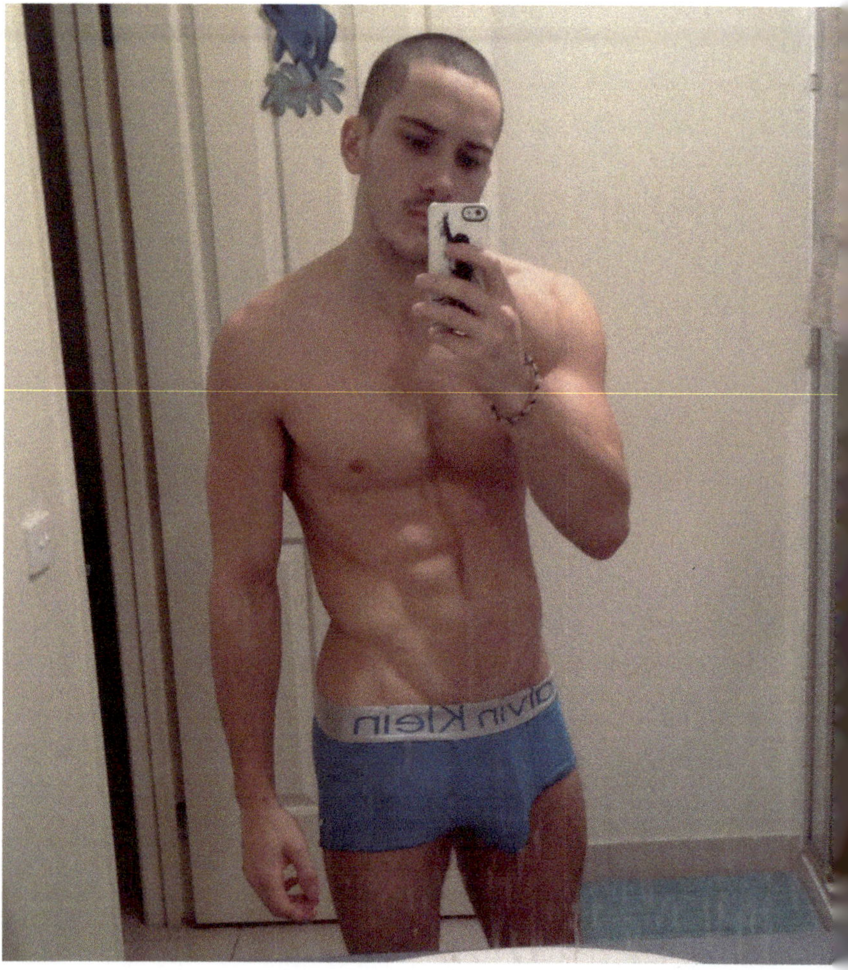

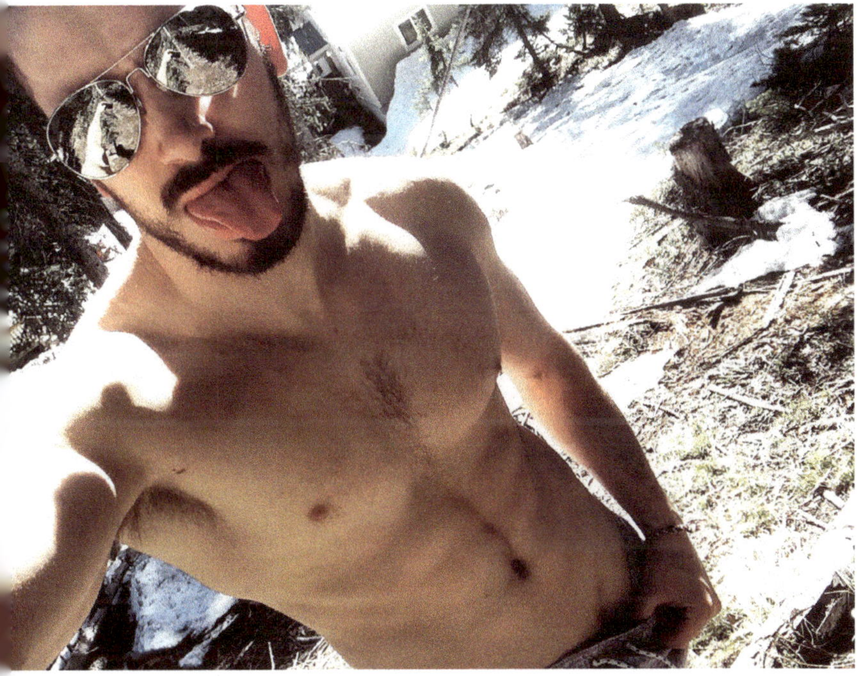

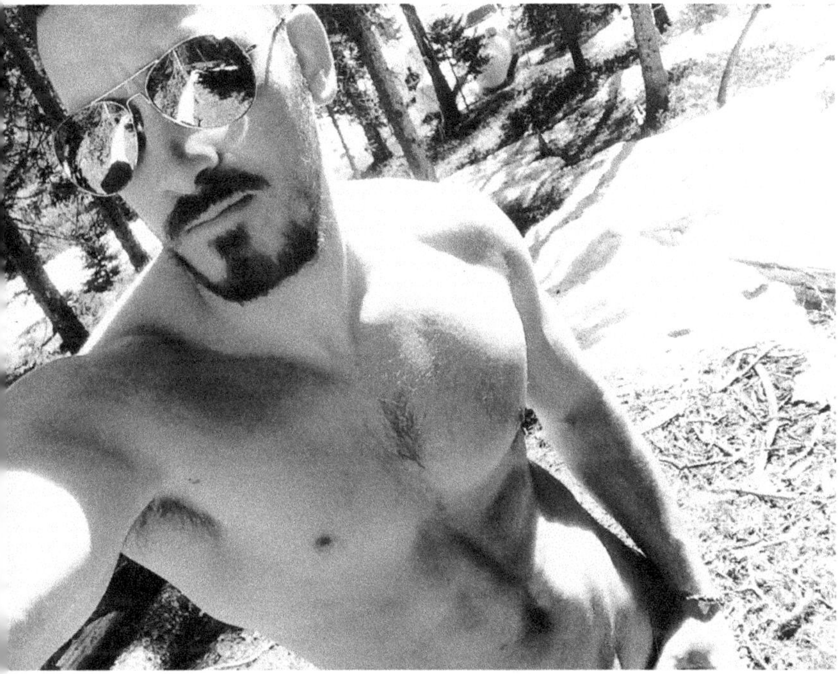

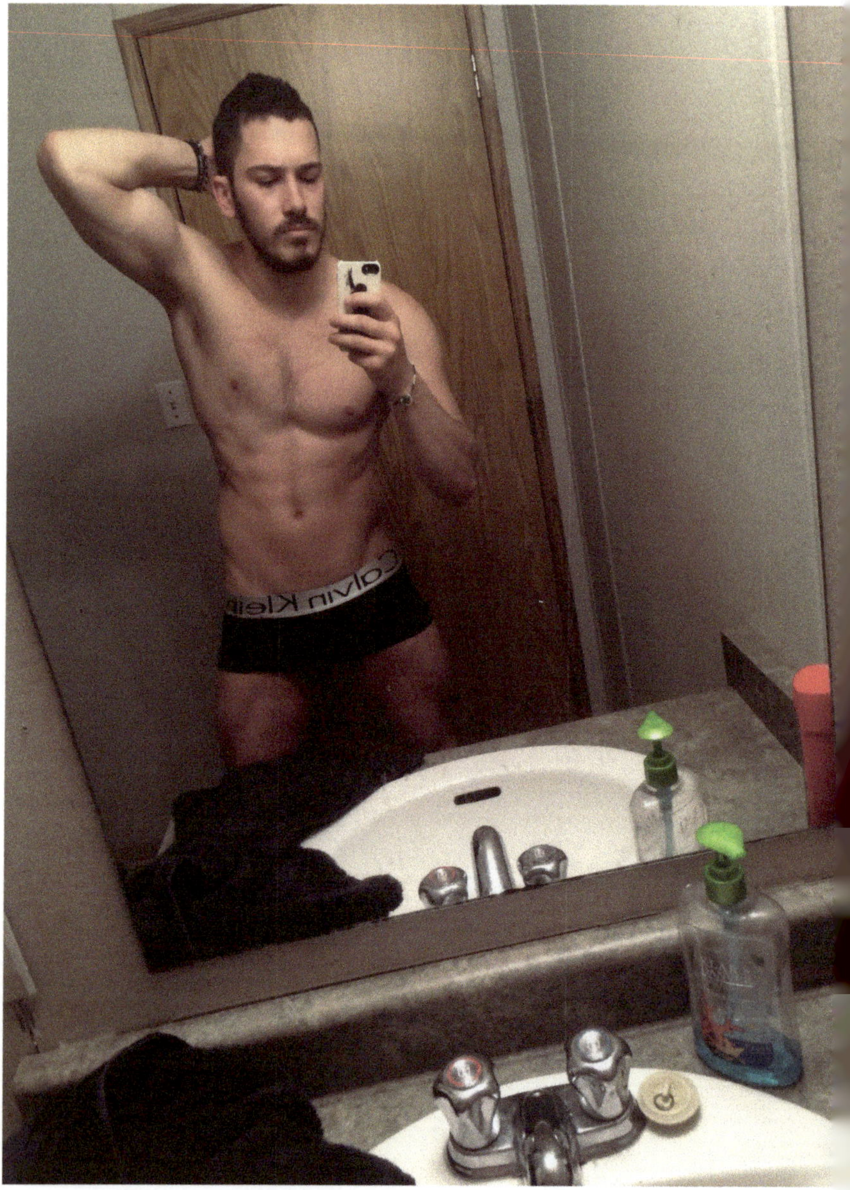

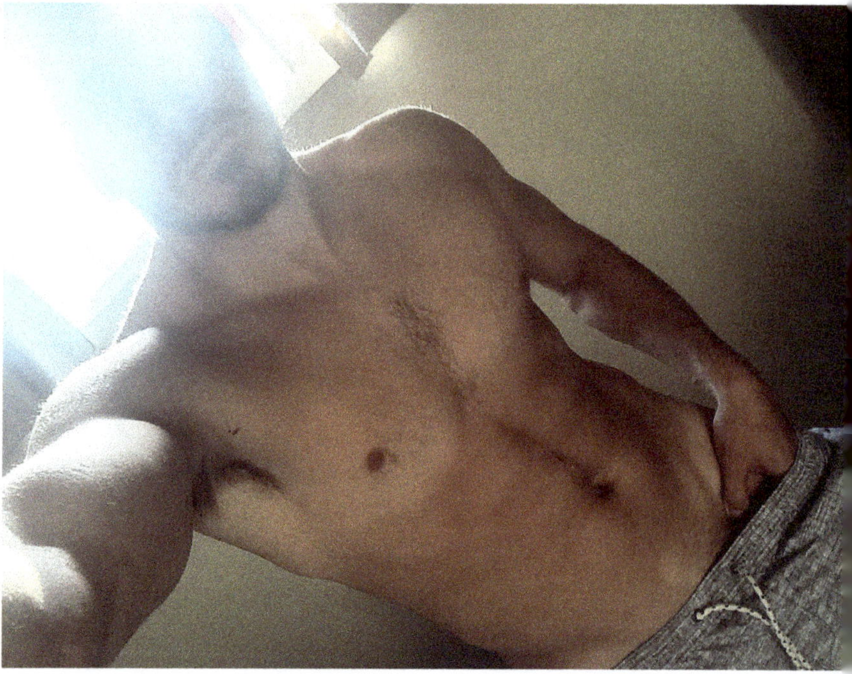

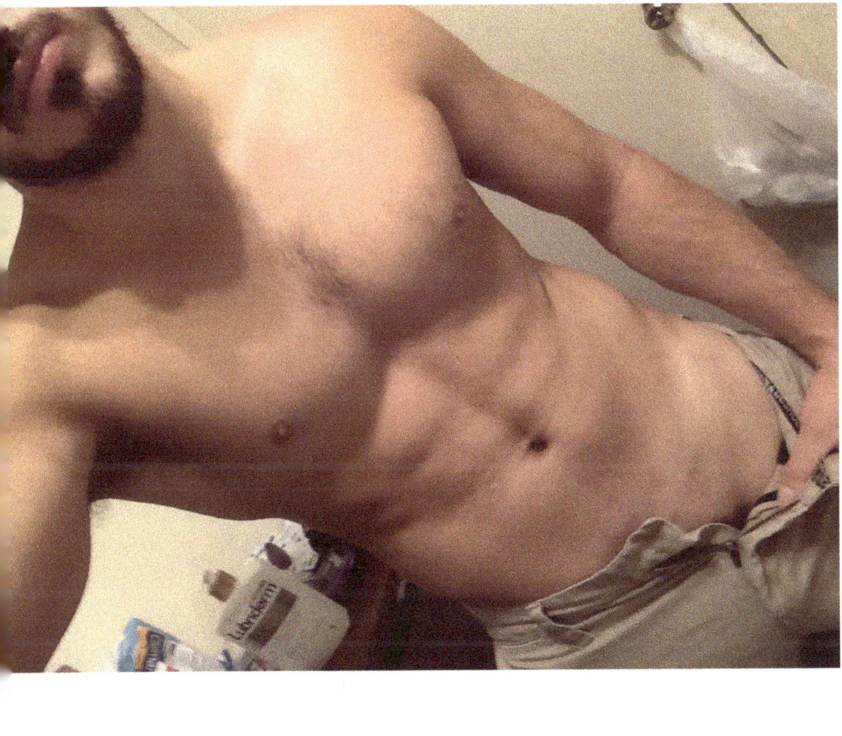
Lubriderm

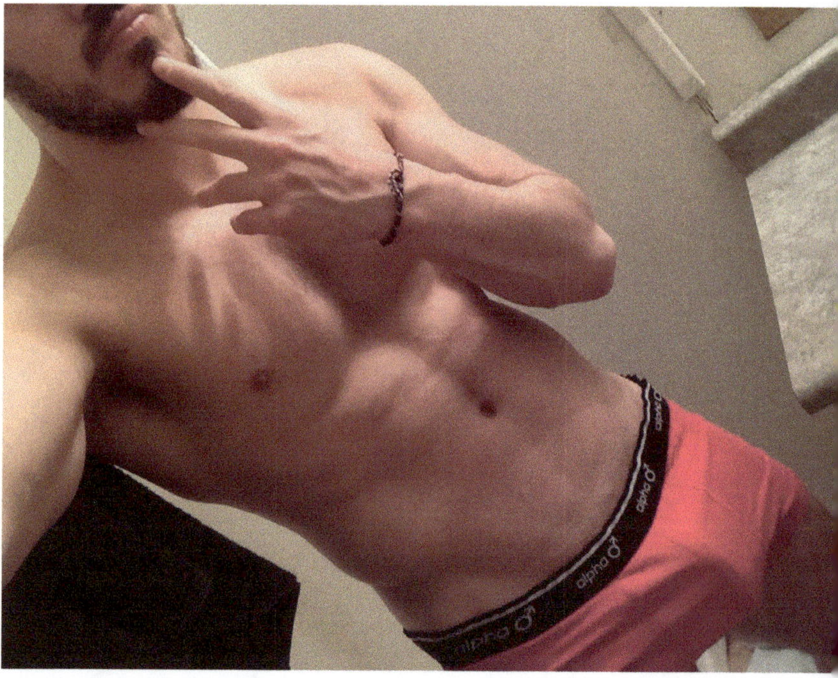
alpha

orona
xtra

Klein

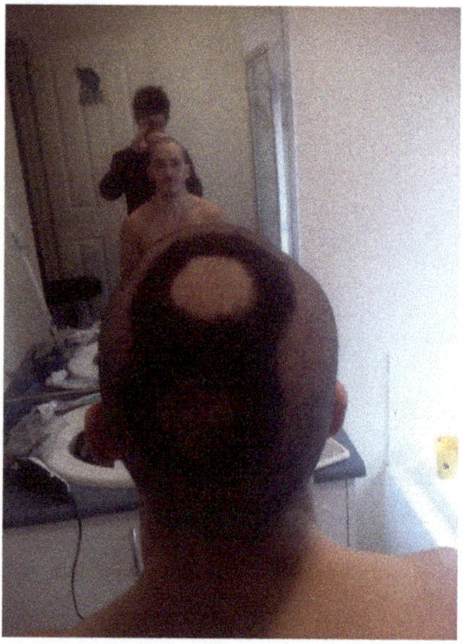

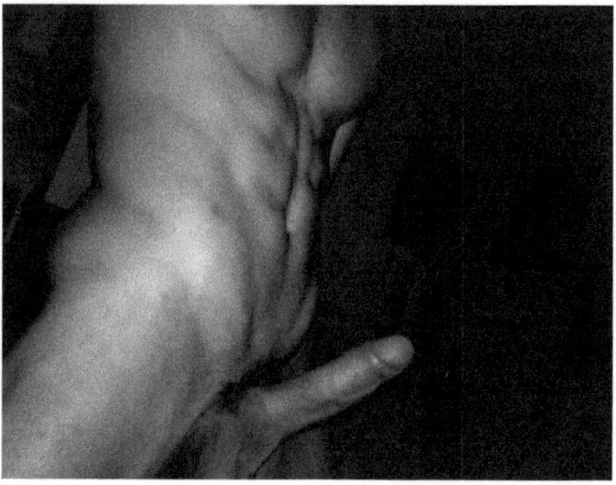

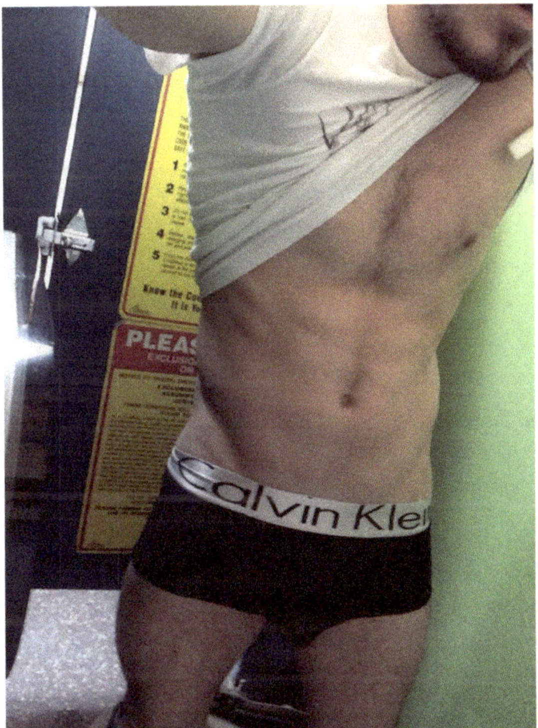
Calvin Kle

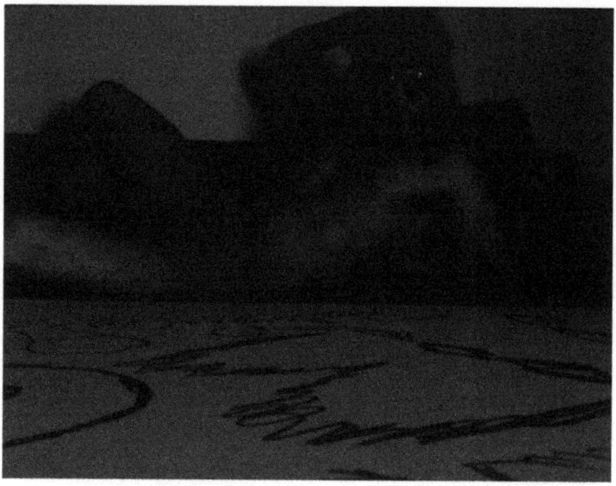

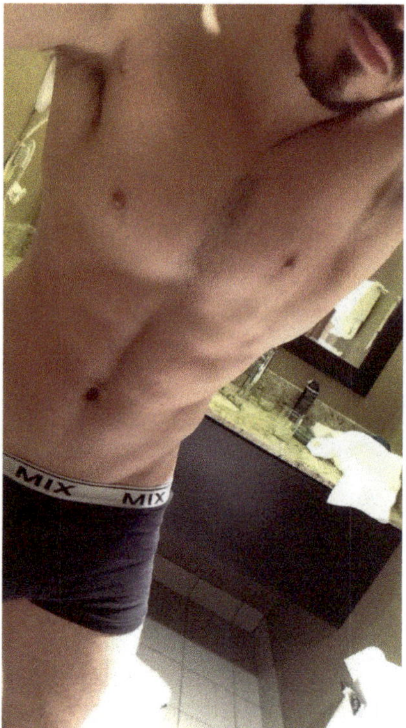
MIX
MIX

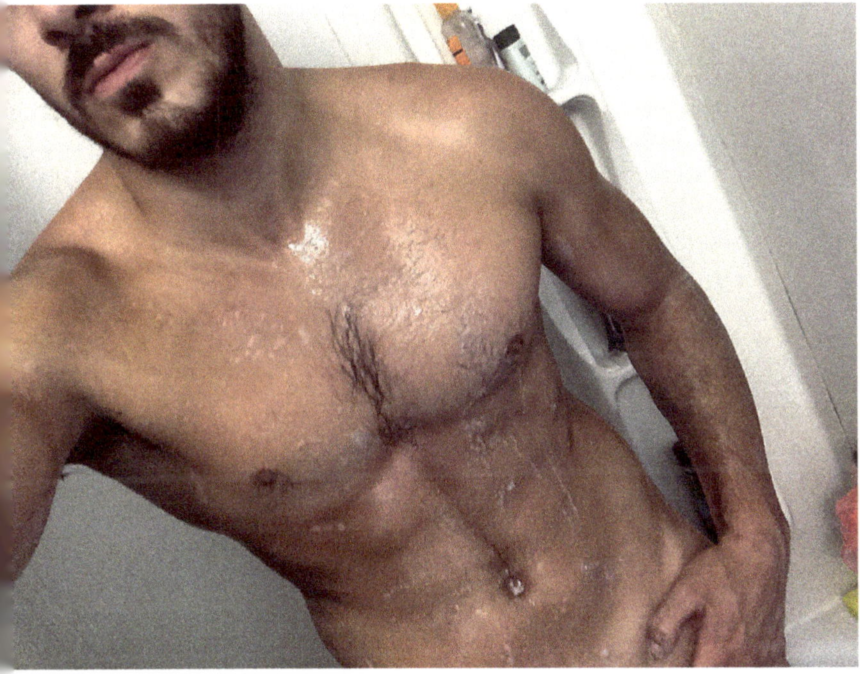

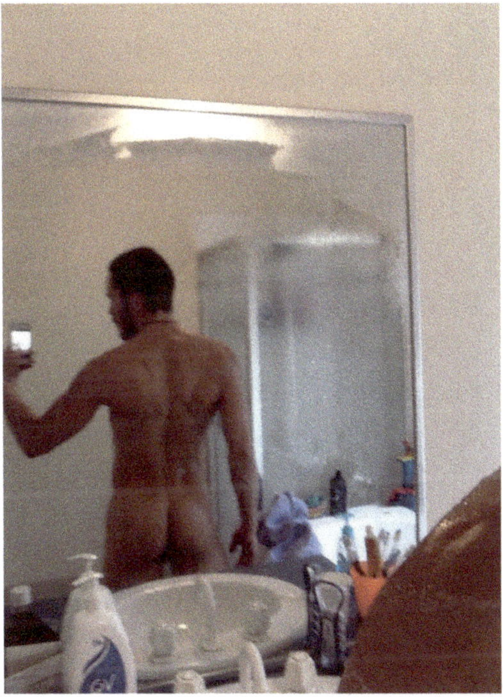

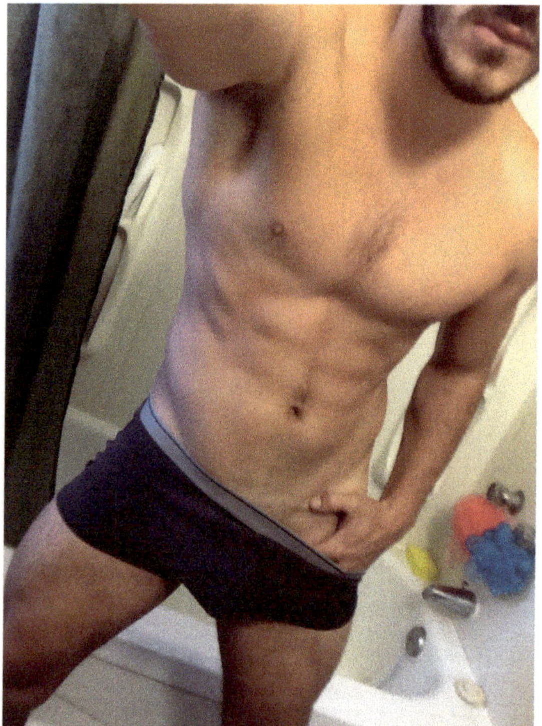

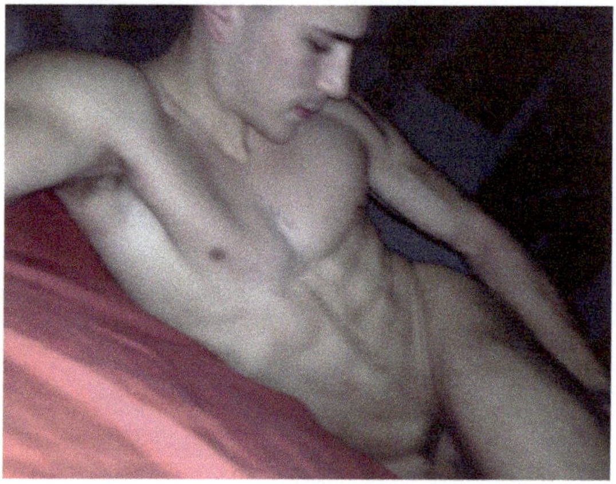

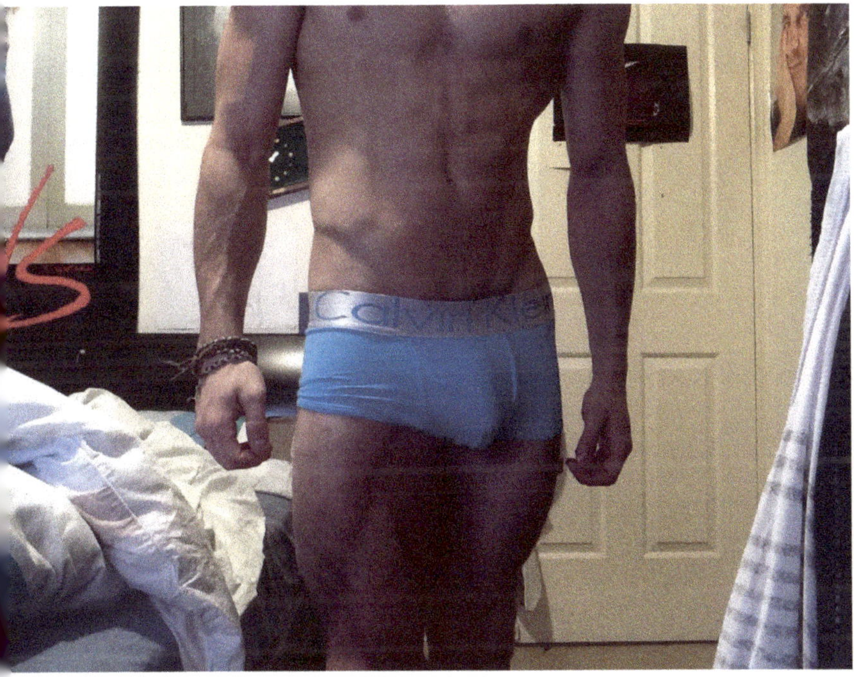

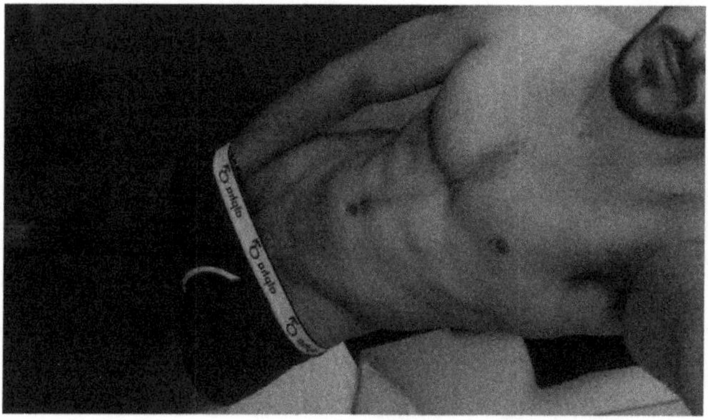

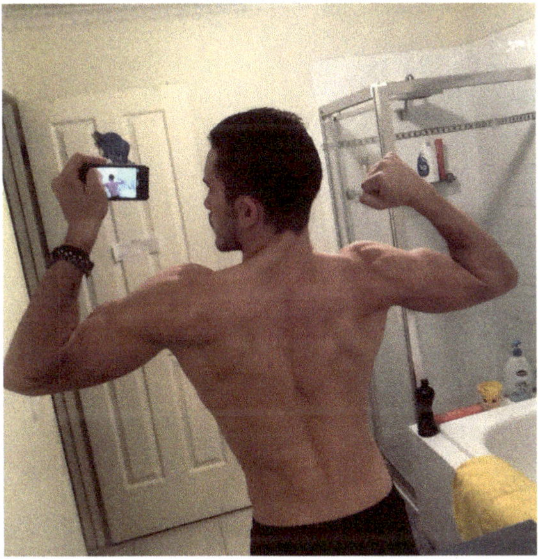

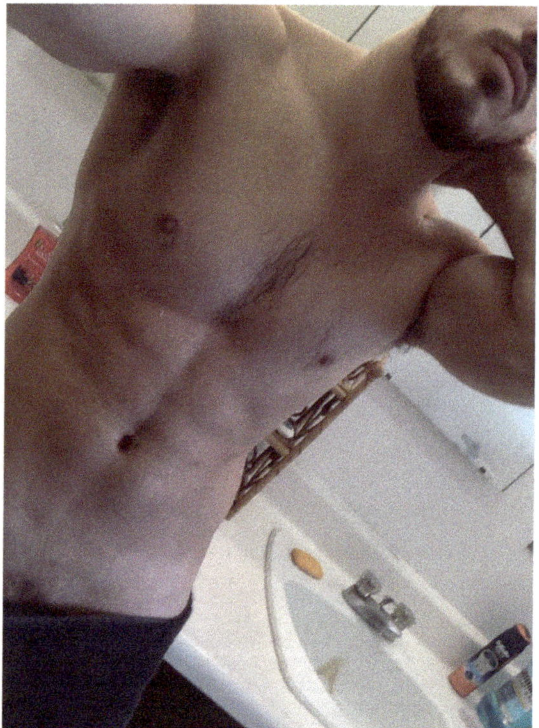

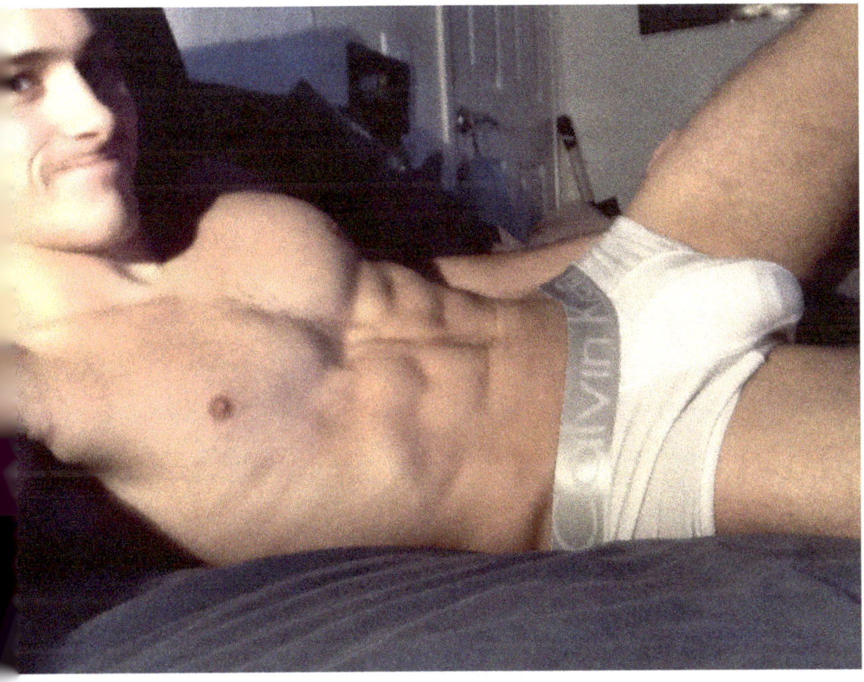

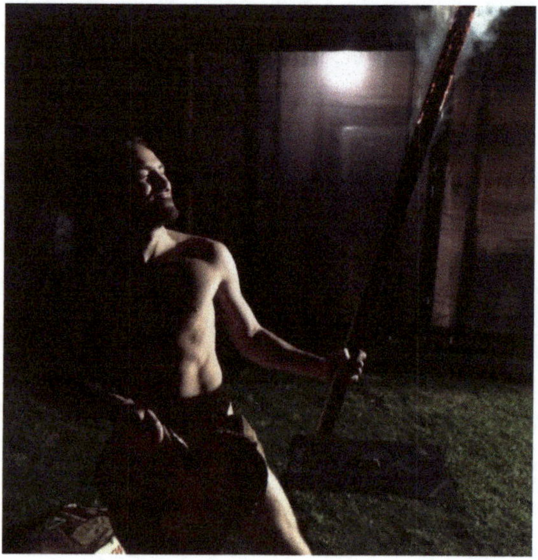

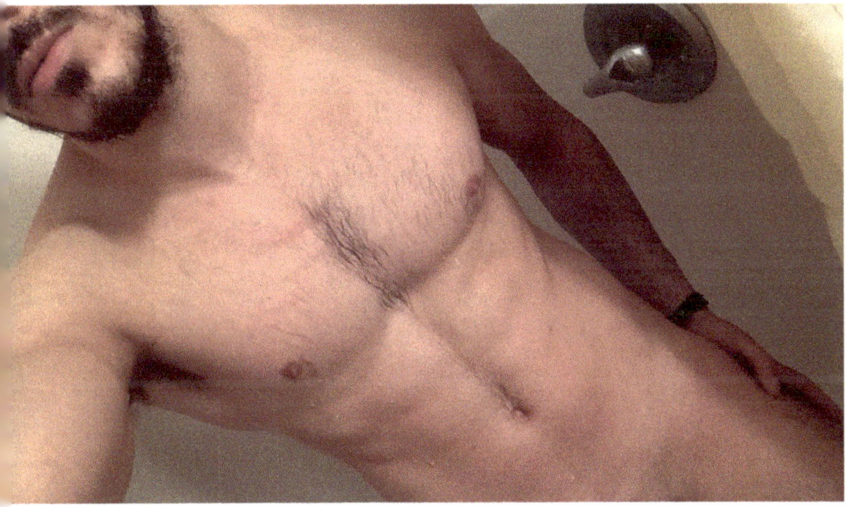

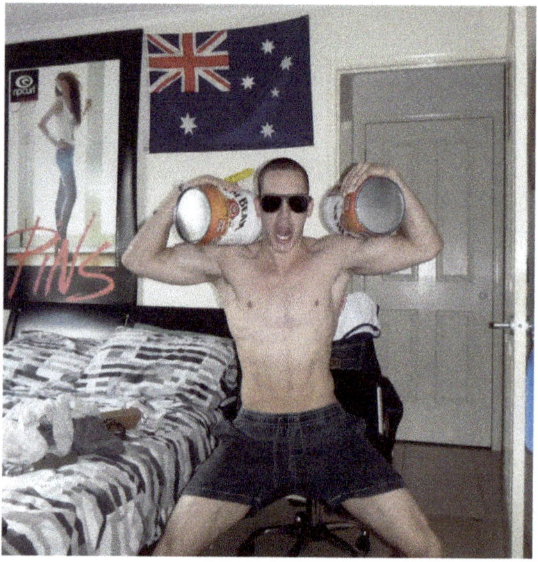
PINS

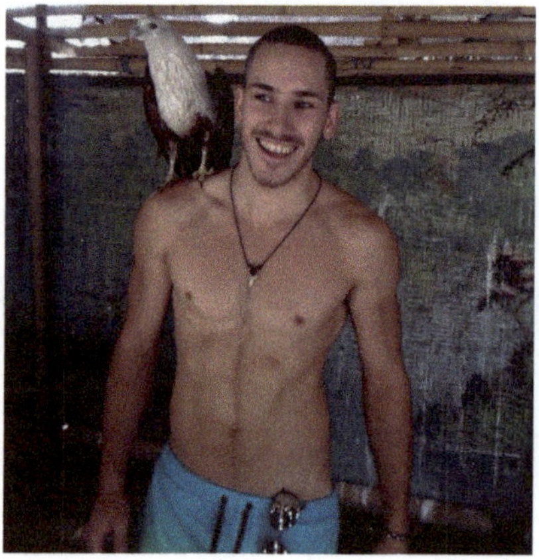

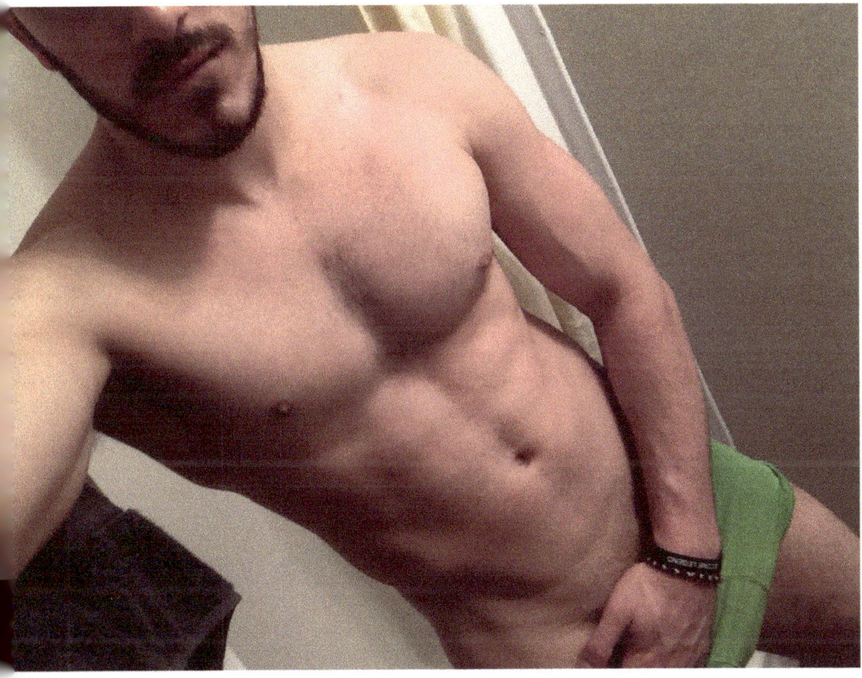

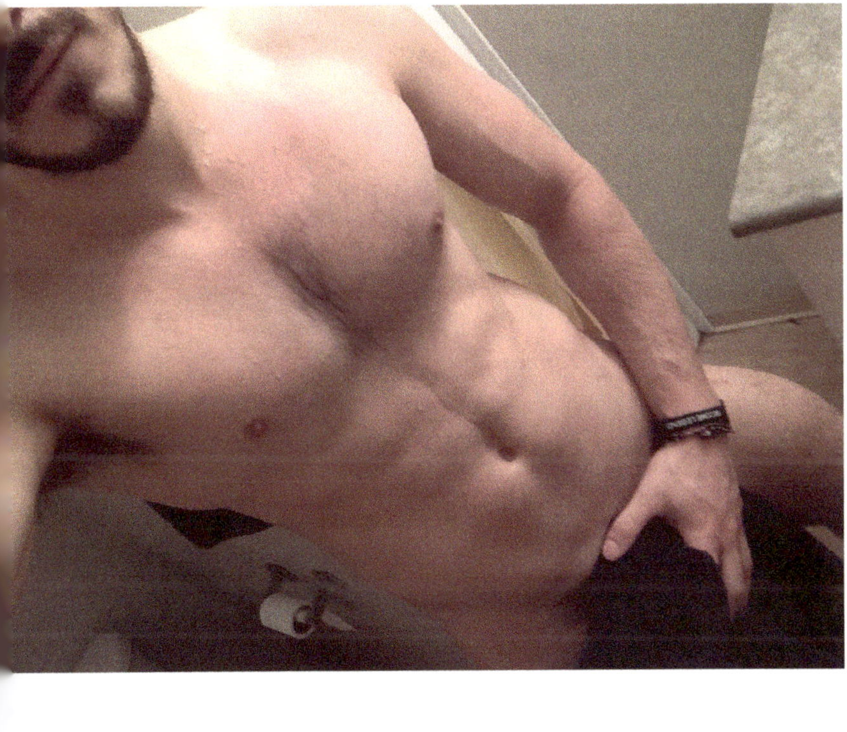

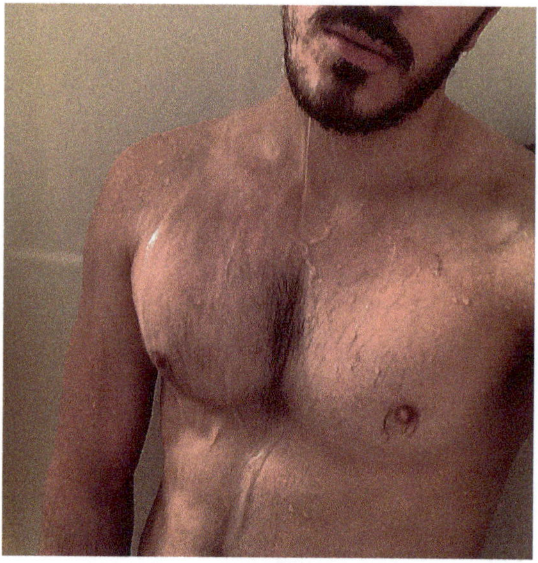

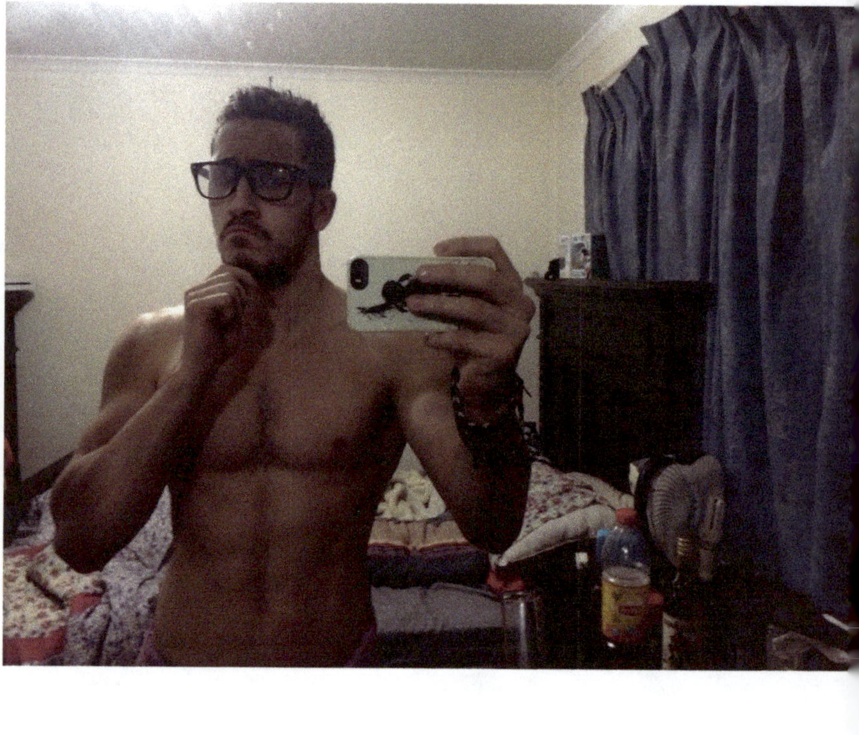

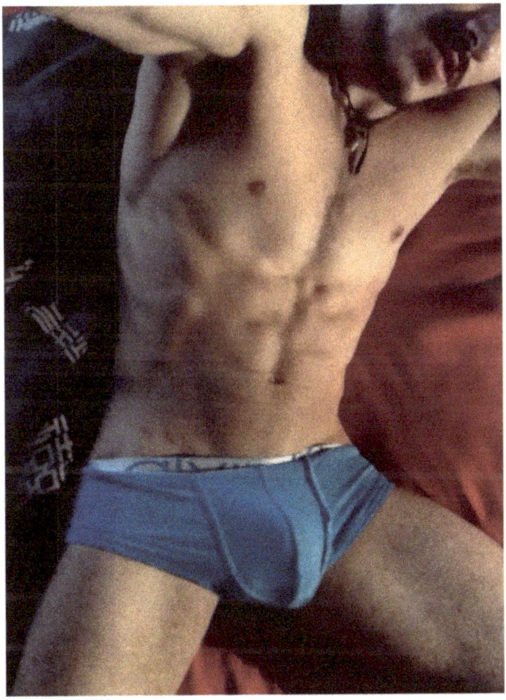

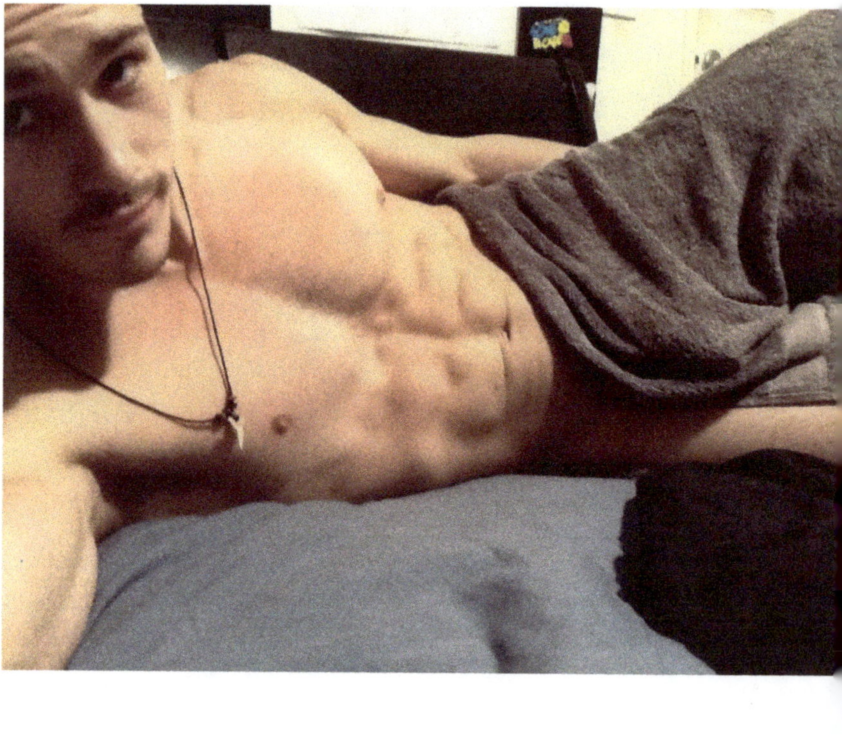

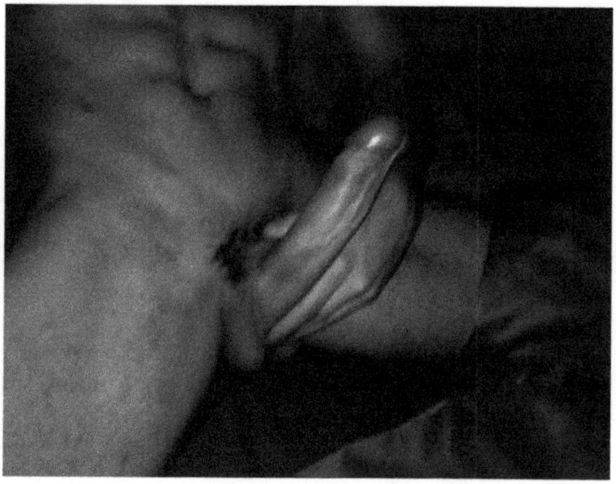

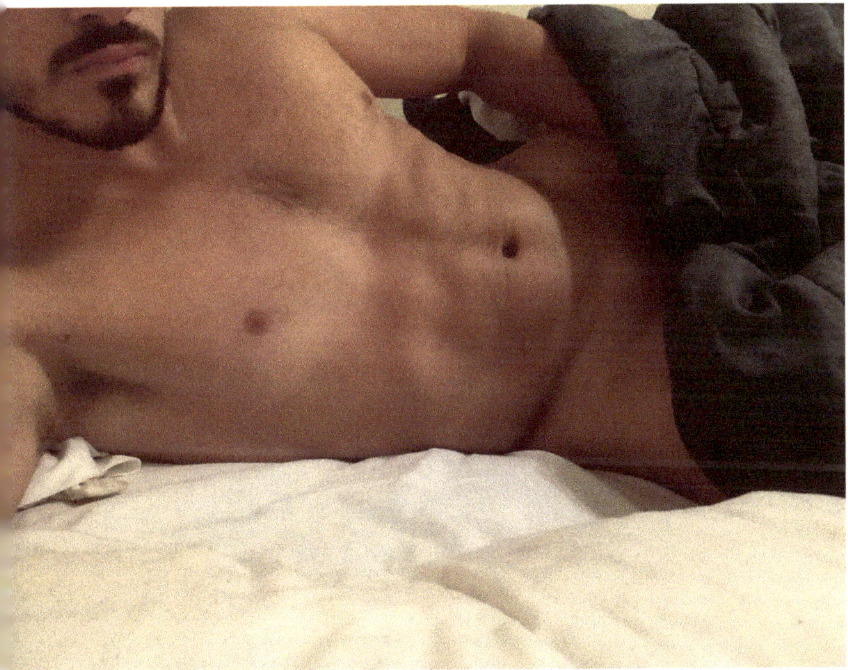

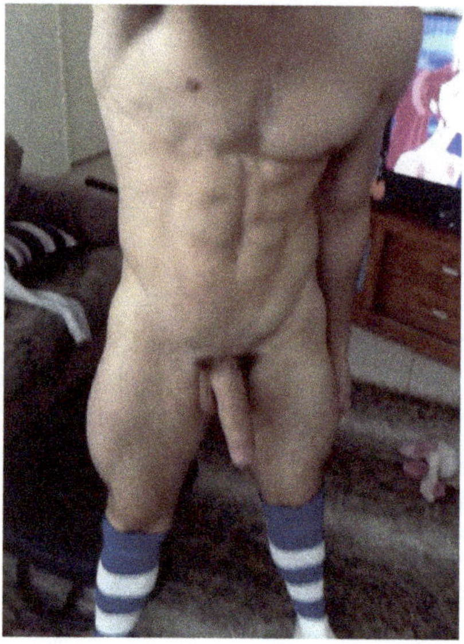

CPSIA information can be obtained
at www.ICGtesting.com
Printed in the USA
BVHW021348140319
542674BV00013B/144/P

9 780368 401947